Mercedes and the Chocolate Pilot

A TRUE STORY OF THE BERLIN AIRLIFT AND THE CANDY THAT DROPPED FROM THE SKY

By Margot Theis Raven

Illustrated by Gijsbert van Frankenhuyzen

To the children of Berlin, the children of the World, and the children of Heaven,
especially Nick Ressler, who knew the power in a stick of gum.

—MTR

To those who preserve our freedom.

—GSH

Text Copyright © 2002 Margot Theis Raven
Illustration Copyright © 2002 Gijsbert van Frankenhuyzen

HERSEY'S Milk Chocolate Bars® is a registered trademark of
Hershey Foods Corporation. All rights reserved. Used with permission.

Sleeping Bear Press™

2395 South Huron Parkway, Suite 200
Ann Arbor, MI 48104
www.sleepingbearpress.com

Printed and bound in the United States.

25 24 23 22 21 20 (case)

Library of Congress Cataloging-in-Publication Data
Raven, Margot Theis.
Mercedes and the Chocolate Pilot / by Margot Theis Raven
p. cm.
Summary: The true story of a young German girl, Mercedes Simon, and of the American pilot Gail Halvorsen, who
shares hope and joy with the children of West Berlin by dropping candy-filled parachutes during the Airlift.

ISBN: 978-1-58536-069-7 case

1. Berlin (Germany)—History—Blockade, 1948-1949—Juvenile literature. 2. Halvorsen, Gail S.—Juvenile literature. 3. United States. Air Force.
Military Airlift Command—Biography—Juvenile literature. 4. Air pilots. Military—United States—Biography—Juvenile literature. 5. Simon,
Mercedes—Juvenile literature. 6. Girls—Germany—Berlin—Biography—Juvenile literature. [1. Berlin (Germany)—History—Blockade, 1948-
1949—Juvenile literature. 2. Halvorsen, Gail S. 3. Simon, Mercedes. 4. United States. Air Force. Military Airlift Command—Biography. 5. Air
Pilots, Military 6. World War, 1939-1945—Germany. 7. Germany—History—1945-1955.] 1. Title.
DD881.R382002   943'.1550874—dc21   2002001887

Additional letters and first-hand accounts of the Chocolate Pilot can be found in his book,
***The Berlin Candy Bomber*. Order information is available at: wigglywings@juno.com**

Further information about Colonel Halvorsen and the Berlin Airlift can be found on the
Berlin Airlift Veterans Association web page at: www.konnections.com/airlift/candy.htm

AUTHOR'S NOTE

This book exists through the generous support and blessings of Col. Gail S. Halvorsen USAF (Ret.) and Mercedes Wild, Berlin, Germany. Thank you both from the depths of my heart for the honor and privilege of telling your story.

Thank you also to the following individuals and friends who went out of their way to help gather and give important information: Peter Wild (Berlin, Germany); Col. Kenneth Herman USAF (Ret.), past-president of the Berlin Airlift Veterans Association; Gudrun Fruehling, president and managing editor, Armed Forces Journal International; Christa Borgman, German language specialist; Ken Sansom; and Karin, Klaus, Marcel, and Frau Lilo Besier, caring neighbors.

Thank you also to my agent, Andrea Brown, for supporting this project from the very beginning, and a heartfelt thank you to my editor, Heather Hughes, associate editor Barb McNally, and publicist Mary Ann Riehle, for believing in the goodness of this story and getting its message out so quickly.

Lastly, a most loving thank you to my brother-in-law, Bob Weed, for your magical touch; my son, Scott, for our Adobe sessions; my husband, Greg, for your loving help in Washington; and most especially to my daughter, Ashley, who shared the book's creation with me, from our trip to Utah to making endless weekends of photocopying so much fun!

—MARGOT THEIS RAVEN

I offer my undying gratitude to my dear friend, Mercedes, and to the exceptional professionals who captured the magic of her struggle to be free: author, Margot Raven; illustrator, Gijsbert van Frankenhuyzen; and team Sleeping Bear Press.

—COLONEL GAIL HALVORSEN

ILLUSTRATOR'S NOTE

As always, I would like to thank the models who helped me with my book. Ustina Treber Shives, a beautiful girl inside and out. You make a wonderful Mercedes. Ben Winkel, actor/body double. From Cornell Elementary, Ron McCurdy's fourth grade class and from Gunnisonville Elementary, John Shives's fifth grade class. Most of all, my gratitude and respect to Colonel Gail Halvorsen and his gracious wife, Lorraine, for sharing their home and hospitality with me. The stories you shared helped make the book what it is. A story of hope, love, and forgiveness.

—GIJSBERT VAN FRANKENHUYZEN

There is no discussion. We stay in Berlin. Period!

President Harry S. Truman
June 28, 1948

THE BERLIN AIRLIFT

The Berlin Airlift of 1948-1949 is still one of the greatest humanitarian missions the world has ever known. Like a great sky bridge, airplanes flew 24 hours a day, three minutes apart, to feed 2.2 million people for 15 desperate months.

It began three years after WWII had ended, when defeated Germany and its capital, Berlin, were carved into four pieces like a pie by the Allied countries who had conquered Adolf Hitler's army. Josef Stalin's Soviet Union (Russia) controlled the eastern sector of Berlin as well as East Germany. Great Britain, the United States, and France controlled the three western sectors of Berlin as well as West Germany.

At first, all four Allies ruled Germany in friendship, but on the fateful day of June 24, 1948, Josef Stalin tried to take both East and West Berlin for himself so he could eventually put all of Germany, then all of Europe, under his communist government. Since Berlin sat 110 miles deep within Russia's territory, Stalin simply had to blockade the roads, railroads, and canal routes coming in and out of the city to cut off West Berliners from food, clothing, heat, and electricity.

What could the Allies do? If they freed West Berlin with guns and tanks there would be another world war! Only three air corridors, each 20 miles wide, were still open for the U.S., Great Britain, and France to utilize. And so the idea for the incredible sky bridge began.

From June 26th, 1948 to September 30th, 1949, the British and American forces flew more than 277, 000 missions, day and night, delivering more than 2.3 million tons of supplies. This is the same distance as going back and forth between the earth and the moon 130 times!

To keep people alive, Berlin needed 4,500 tons of food, coal, and essentials daily! Imagine packing, carrying, and unloading 646 tons of flour and wheat per day; 180 tons of dehydrated potatoes; 19 tons of powdered milk; 5 tons of fresh milk for babies and small children; 109 tons of meat and fat; 125 tons of cereal; and combined, over 5,000 tons of coal and kerosene during the summer and winter. And many other essential items were part of the cargo!

Nothing was easy about this rescue mission and there were many problems: the weather was terrible; the runways short; the skies crowded; the pilots had little sleep; Russian planes harassed the exhausted fliers in the air corridors; coal and flour dust caused mechanical problems.

The greatest cost of the operation was the loss of lives: 31 Americans died, 39 British, and 9 Germans. But they are not forgotten. In Berlin today, the memory of the beautiful "bridge" is cherished by the people who love their freedom, and remember the brave pilots and the countries who did not forsake them in their time of need.

This is the true story of a seven-year-old girl named Mercedes Simon who lived in the city of West Berlin during the airlift and of the American pilot who came to be known as the Chocolate Pilot.

BERLIN 1948

One late August day, Mercedes slipped her hand under the white chickens she kept in the small courtyard garden behind her apartment building.

Please let there be eggs, she wished as the silver-winged planes flew above like guardian angels. But like yesterday and the day before, the chickens' nests were empty, except for one small egg.

Mercedes fed each chicken a worm and tried not to cry. She loved her four feathered pets, but Mama would not be happy. Eggs were more precious than gold in West Berlin during the Russian blockade.

"Tomorrow I want an egg from each of you," she scolded the chickens sternly, "or Mama will say we cannot afford to keep you and must have you for dinner instead!"

Walking up the bomb-splintered steps to her apartment, Mercedes was sure her white chickens were just too scared of the thundering planes of the airlift to lay their eggs.

Night and day they roared overhead like huge silver birds into nearby Tempelhof Air Field to unload their supplies. But Mercedes would never complain about the great soaring grocery stores that everyone called *Raisinbombers*, because they carried yummy raisins to eat! They carried flour and clothing and coal too. And something else!

One day Mama read her a newspaper story about
the candy that came from the planes. The story
told about the wonderful American Chocolate
Pilot, Lt. Gail Halvorsen. Every day, he
rained down sweets on the children
who cheered the planes landing
on Tempelhof's runway.

As Mama read, Mercedes learned how the tall, friendly pilot had talked with these children one day at the fence near the runway's end.

"The children didn't ask him for candy," Mama read, "only sweet freedom. Still, before he had to go, he searched his pocket for gum. But he found only two sticks—and there were 30 children!"

"What did he do, Mama?" Mercedes asked.

"He split the sticks for four lucky children," Mama read, "and the others tore slivers of the foil to smell as their sweet treats. Then, even though he knew he could get in terrible trouble, the pilot promised the children he would drop gum and candy to them from his plane the next day! He stretched out his arms and told them to look for the wiggle of his plane's wings."

"That night the pilot made small candy-filled parachutes from handkerchiefs," Mama read on, "and dropped them in secret to the children at the airfield the next day. He made three candy drops after that, before his troubles began!"

"Children's letters addressed to *The Chocolate Pilot* and *Uncle Wiggly Wings* began to arrive at the airfield. Then a candy bar almost hit a reporter on his head, and the colonel in charge at Tempelhof read about the pilot's secret in the newspaper! He was caught!"

"Did the colonel yell at him?" Mercedes cringed, but Mama laughed and said, "Only a little, then he shook his hand and told him to 'keep dropping and keep him informed!'"

"But won't he run out of candy?" Mercedes asked anxiously, but Mama laughed again.

"People from all over America now send the pilot handkerchiefs for parachutes, and so much candy that it fills two large railroad boxcars!"

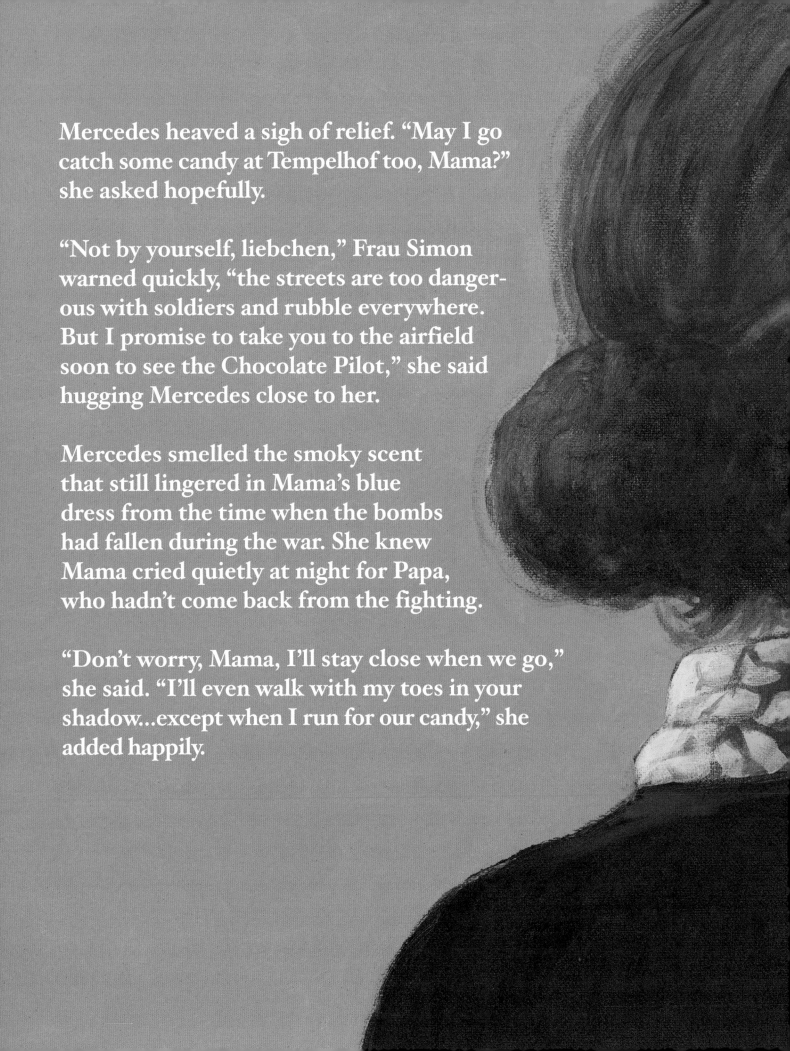

Mercedes heaved a sigh of relief. "May I go catch some candy at Tempelhof too, Mama?" she asked hopefully.

"Not by yourself, liebchen," Frau Simon warned quickly, "the streets are too danger-ous with soldiers and rubble everywhere. But I promise to take you to the airfield soon to see the Chocolate Pilot," she said hugging Mercedes close to her.

Mercedes smelled the smoky scent that still lingered in Mama's blue dress from the time when the bombs had fallen during the war. She knew Mama cried quietly at night for Papa, who hadn't come back from the fighting.

"Don't worry, Mama, I'll stay close when we go," she said. "I'll even walk with my toes in your shadow...except when I run for our candy," she added happily.

A few weeks later, as Mama promised,
Mercedes stood at the airfield fence
with the other hopeful children.
Above her, thundering planes
dropped out of the clouds,

shaking the ground at her feet. Then a great cheer came up from the children when they spotted the wiggle of the Chocolate Pilot's wings! Suddenly, many small white parachutes floated down like marshmallow clouds!

Mercedes ran excitedly with the other children,
with her hands stretched high to capture the
prize in the sky. But at the very
last second, a large boy nearby
reached up a little higher
and grabbed the
parachute drifting
toward her!

And oh, the look in his eyes as he
bit into the silky, smooth chocolate!
It was all Mercedes could think about
the whole sad way home.

That night, listening to the sound of the planes' engines above her home, Mercedes wiped at tears. If only she had caught the chocolate it wouldn't matter if the chickens laid eggs. The candy would make her and Mama so happy! But what could she do?

Then Mercedes remembered from the newspaper that children wrote letters to the Chocolate Pilot. With the moon as her lamp, she got out of bed to write one too. Carefully, as she had learned in school, she penned:

Dear Chocolate Pilot,

"We live near the airfield at Tempelhof, and our chickens think your airplanes are chicken hawks so they become frightened when you fly over to land. They run in shelter and some moult with no more eggs from them. It is a big problem for us. We need the eggs. But when you fly over the garden and see the white chickens, please drop some candy there and all will be ok. I don't care if you scare them."

Your little friend,
Mercedes

Frau Simon mailed Mercedes's letter the next day, quietly keeping the thought behind her lips that such a busy pilot didn't have time to make every child's dream come true.

But Mercedes now waited in the garden with the white chickens every day, wishing on each angel-plane above, for her candy to fall from the sky.

Returning to Rhein-Main Air Force Base in Frankfurt, where he slept and ate between his three round-trip flights into Berlin each day, Lt. Gail Halvorsen put down a handful of letters on his cot. It was late October. For months now, children's letters with crayon-colored drawings arrived for him from all over Berlin. Each week, the many letters were translated by two German secretaries and given to Lt. Halvorsen. A few got his personal reply. But all the letters touched his heart—some even made Lt. Halvorsen laugh 'til he cried.

A nine-year-old boy, Peter Zimmerman, wrote the Chocolate Pilot that his legs were too short to run fast for the candy, so he drew him a map to his house and instructed:

"Fly along the big canal...at the second bridge, turn right...I live in the bombed-out house on the corner. I'll be in the backyard every day at 2 p.m. Drop it there."

Lt. Halvorsen tried to find Peter's house from the sky, but when he couldn't, he boxed up candy bars and gum and sent them to Peter's address by West Berlin Post— but not before he'd heard from Peter again saying, "No chocolate yet! You're a pilot. I gave you a map! How did you guys win the war, anyway?"

Now on this late October day, Lt. Halvorsen quietly opened today's letters. One by one he read them. Then he lingered over a letter from a little girl with white chickens in her courtyard garden. He smiled and laughed and fought back a tear as he read: *We need the eggs. But when you fly over the garden and see the white chickens, please drop some candy there and all will be ok...Your little friend, Mercedes*

Lt. Halvorsen softly rubbed his head. His little friend's sweet hope was as fragile as the eggs and as precious to him as the white chickens were to her. But would he ever find the garden with the chickens? Even with Peter's map, he couldn't find his yard by the canal.

As October days passed into November, a thick, soupy fog
began to blanket Berlin's sky. Walking home with Mama,
Mercedes prayed the pilots would be safe today. She prayed,
too, that the fog would lift so the Chocolate Pilot could find
her chickens in the yard at last.

No candy had rained down yet—maybe he had
stopped looking for the chickens!

PLEASE don't forget me, Mercedes
whispered to the white sky above.

Frau Simon saw the troubled
look on Mercedes's face.
She squeezed her little
hand with love, but
said nothing.

But once inside their apartment at 15 Hahnelstrasse, Frau Simon couldn't wait to give Mercedes the surprise that had come for her earlier that day. It was a package mailed from Tempelhof Air Field, all neatly wrapped in brown paper and tied with string. Quickly, Mercedes tore into the package.

As she opened the box, the sweet smell of
candy spread thick as jam through the room.

Chocolate bars! Packs of white and green mint gum!
Pink bubble gum too! And Life Saver rolls, colored
like the rainbow! Her Chocolate Pilot had
found her at last!

Mercedes saw Mama blinking
back happy tears. She gave
her a thick chocolate
bar to eat, and chose
a creamy bar with
nuts and caramel
nougat for herself.

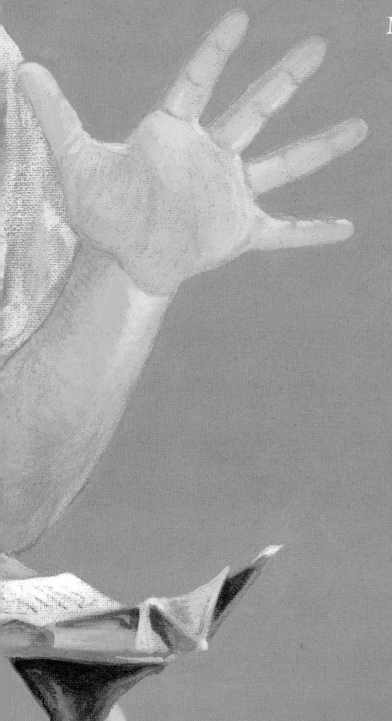

She slipped off its wrapper and peeled back the silver foil. Little by little, she bit into the dark sweetness, letting the smooth taste melt away on her tongue. With each silky bite, she closed her eyes for a second as if she had just tasted heaven.

Inside the box was a letter for Mercedes:

"Meine liebe Mercedes (My dear Mercedes),
Frankfurt, den 4 Nov. 48

"Thank you for your small letter. Not every day I fly over your home, but surely often. I didn't know that in Hahnelstrasse there lived such a nice little girl. If I could fly a few rounds over Friedenau, I surely would find the garden with the white chickens, but for this there is not enough time. I hope that through what is with this letter, I give you a little joy."

Dein Schokoladenonkel,
(Your Chocolate Uncle)
Gail Halvorsen

The memory of this day
would stay with her for
the rest of her life.

A few months later in January of 1949,
Lt. Halvorsen thought of little Mercedes and
Peter Zimmerman and all the children in Berlin
as he flew out of Tempelhof for the very last time.
It didn't seem possible that his seven-month tour
of duty in the Berlin Airlift had ended. He was sad
to go, but as the clouds parted toward America he
smiled, knowing his candy drops to the children
would go on with the help of trusted pilot friends.

What Lt. Halvorsen didn't know that day, was that
his story in Berlin wasn't over....

Epilogue

In 1970, 22 years later, Colonel Gail S. Halvorsen, the Chocolate Pilot, returned to Berlin with his wife and five children. Now *he* was the new colonel in charge at Tempelhof and the U.S. Air Force representative to Berlin!

One night in 1972, Col. Halvorsen accepted a dinner invitation from a Berlin couple whom he had never met. A young mother of two boys greeted him warmly at an old apartment building near Tempelhof Air Field. The young woman was also a pilot.

From her china cabinet where she kept her treasures, she took out a letter. "Please read this," she said to Col. Halvorsen. The letter began: "Meine liebe Mercedes."

"I ate the candy little by little," Mercedes's smile quivered as her eyes welled with tears of love and gratitude, "but I will keep the letter forever."

Mercedes showed Col. Halvorsen the window where she had watched the planes and showed him the yard below where the white chickens had once lived. Then she tried to tell him how much his gift had meant to her.

Col. Halvorsen's eyes misted over. Oh, yes, he knew! But how could he tell Mercedes the joy that had come to him from two sticks of gum? He'd seen a World War go by, and a Cold War begin, but he'd always found in the children's eyes the hope for a better tomorrow. No, he couldn't explain, so he penned a wish for Mercedes on his original letter:

Dear Mercedes and family!   *22 SEPT 1972*

I am very happy to greet you and your wonderful family after 24 years. I wish you the best future possible with many sweet things to come!

Gail S. Halvorsen

For many years, Mercedes kept the letter in her china cabinet, and each time he visited her, Col. Halvorsen left a new message of friendship on it.

The letter, still Mercedes's most precious possession, is now kept in a bank vault, and is only brought out when her beloved Chocolate Pilot comes to visit once more.

But every day when Mercedes walks under the skies of a free Berlin, the sweet memory of his gift still soars in her heart like the great silver planes of hope.

LT. HALVORSEN'S wonderful *Operation Little Vittles*, as the candy drops came to be called, grew into a worldwide mission of love. The people of Chicopee, Massachusetts, hearing about Gail's work on the radio, took up his cause. Using an old fire station as the center for Little Vittles, leaders organized local businesses and 22 schools to supply: 11,000 yards of ribbons; 2,000 sheets for chutes; 3,000 handkerchiefs; and 18 tons of candy and gum. At peak production, 800 pounds of candy-tied parachutes were shipped to Rhein-Main every other day!

By January 1949, when Lt. Gail Halvorsen left Berlin, he'd flown 126 airlift missions and in all, during the 15 months of the blockade, Gail and his squadron dropped more than 250,000 candy-loaded parachutes, more than 20 tons of chocolate and gum to Berlin's 100,000 children, such as his beloved Mercedes.

In 1974, Colonel Gail S. Halvorsen retired from the U.S. Air Force after 31 years of service and many, many humanitarian honors. Today, Gail divides his time between a ranch in Utah and a home in Arizona, and still makes candy drops to children all over the world. During his many visits to Berlin, he has rained down candy to the children and grandchildren of the original Berliners at the fence. He has flown candy to refugee camps in Bosnia in 1994 and in 1999 to Camp Hope, the U.S.-built shelter for Albanians fleeing from Kosovo. Gail has also rained his sky-candy on his own 24 grandchildren, and to the four children of Mercedes and her husband, Peter Wild.

Colonel Gail S. Halvorsen, 2002

MARGOT THEIS RAVEN has been a professional writer working in the fields of radio, television, magazines, newspapers, and children's books for 30 years. She has won five national awards, including an IRA Teacher's Choice award. Margot earned her degree in English from Rosemont College and attended Villanova University for theater study, and Kent State University for German language. The mother of four children (and three dogs), Margot is married and lives in Charleston, SC, and West Chesterfield, NH.

As a writer of historical fiction, Margot came across a story about a retired U.S. Air Force Colonel named Gail Halvorsen who had parachuted candy down to children during the Berlin Airlift. She was hooked right away to learn everything she could about this wonderful pilot and his postwar work. Soon after, she and her daughter flew to Utah to meet the Colonel and his family. From that meeting a beautiful friendship began, and the great adventure of bringing his unique story of hope and love to today's children.

GIJSBERT VAN FRANKENHUYZEN was born in the Netherlands in 1951. Together with seven brothers and sisters, he grew up during a time when the country was still showing the effects of World War II. Always drawing as a young boy, his father encouraged Gijsbert to make art his career. After high school, he attended and graduated from the Royal Academy of Arts in Arnhem. He immigrated to America in 1976 and worked as art director for the Michigan Natural Resources Magazine for 17 years. Gijsbert now paints full-time and loves the freedom of painting whatever he wants.

Gijsbert and Robbyn and daughters, Kelly and Heather, share their 40-acre farm with sheep, horses, dogs, cats, turkeys, rabbits, chickens, and pigeons. They also provide a temporary home for many orphaned and injured wildlife. The farm, the land, and the animals make great subjects for the artist to paint.

Gijsbert felt the best part of working on *Mercedes and the Chocolate Pilot* was meeting Colonel Gail Halvorsen and his gracious wife, Lorraine. "He is the kindest and most admirable person I have ever met, and I am proud to know him."